The Assyrian and Neo-Assyrian Empire

Children's Middle Eastern History Books

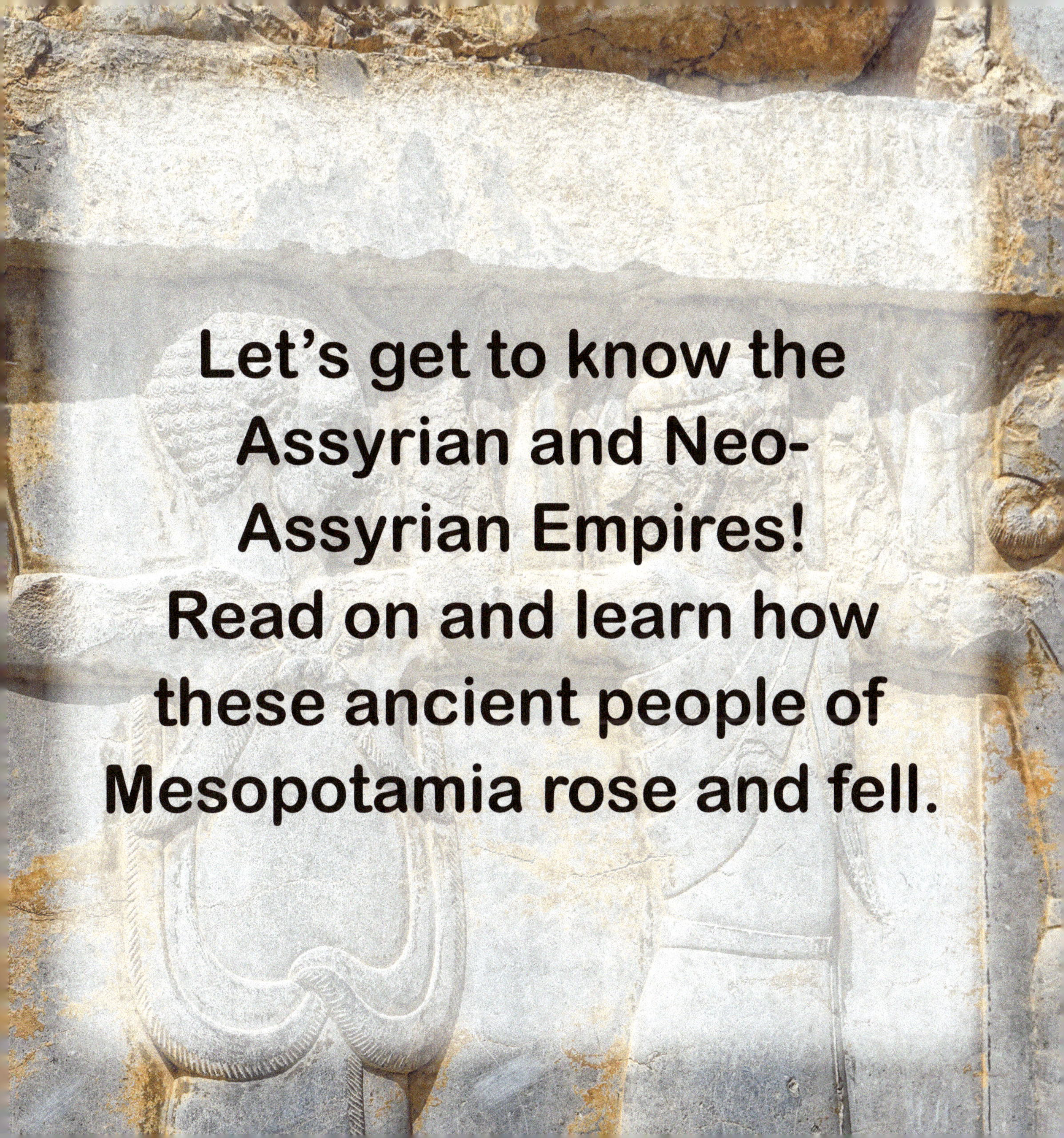

Let's get to know the Assyrian and Neo-Assyrian Empires!
Read on and learn how these ancient people of Mesopotamia rose and fell.

We'll start with
the amazing
Assyrian Empire!

The Rise of the Assyrian Empire

The Assyrians
were warlike
people. They were
also great traders.
They traveled to
different places
and cities in
Mesopotamia to
sell their goods
such as food
and wine.

The Assyrians spoke their own language. They shared and worshiped the gods worshiped by the Sumerians and Babylonians.

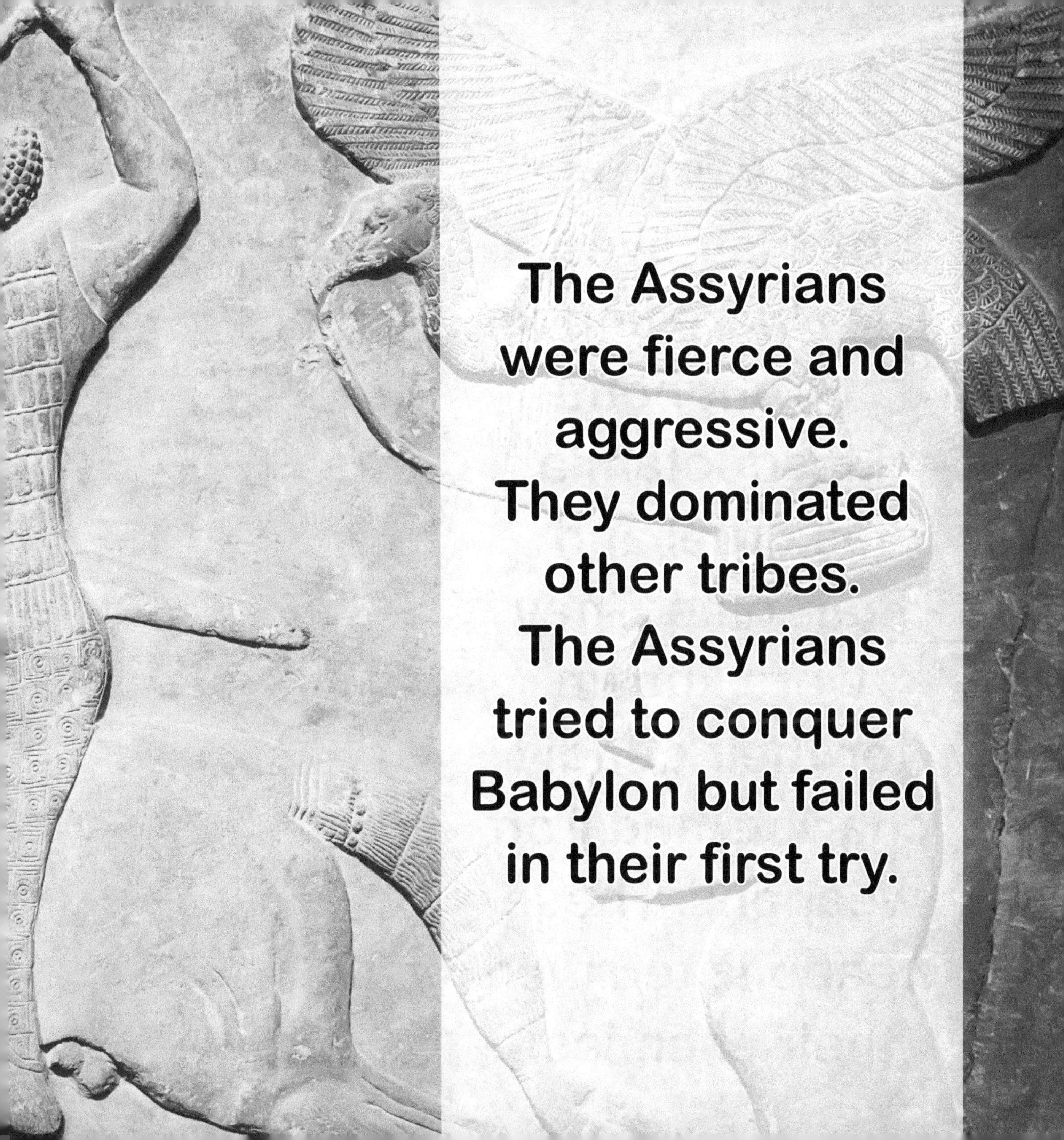
The Assyrians
were fierce and
aggressive.
They dominated
other tribes.
The Assyrians
tried to conquer
Babylon but failed
in their first try.

Fighting and wars were part of their lives. They were known throughout Mesopotamia as cruel and fearsome. They were known for their deadly chariots and iron weapons. These weapons terrified their enemies.

The Assyrians patiently waited for the right time to attack the city of Babylon again. When the Assyrians were ready for battle, they conquered all the cities and the whole of the Babylonian Empire in 1200 BCE. The Assyrians destroyed the city of Babylon.

The city of Babylon was built in honor of the powerful god Marduk. When the Assyrians realized this, they feared that Marduk would get angry.

As a result, the Assyrians rebuilt the city of Babylon. However, the city remained empty for a long time. The Assyrians did not let anyone settle in the beautiful, but empty, city.

Shamshi-Adad. He was one of the strongest and powerful Assyrian leaders. He worked hard to help the Assyrian Empire expand. Under his reign, the Assyrians became rich. His death led to the downfall of the Assyrians at the hands of the Babylonians.

King Tiglath-Pileser I.
When he became the leader, the Assyrians were able to conquer Mesopotamia, including the rich and powerful city of Babylon.

King Ashurbanipal.
He was the last great
Assyrian leader. Durng
his reign, he built
the famous library at
the city of Nineveh.
It was called the
Library at Nineveh.

Neo-Assyrian Empire. This is one of the strongest empires in the world. It flourished from 744 BC to 612 BC. The brave and powerful rulers of the neo-Assyrian Empire included Tiglath –Pileser III, Sargon II, Sennacherib, and Ashurbanipal. They helped the neo-Assyrian Empire become one of the strongest empires in the whole world.

However, in 612 BC, the Assyrian Empire fell apart under attacks by the rising Babylonians.

Among the
great cities of
the Assyrian
Empire were
Ashur, Nimrud,
and Nineveh.

The capital of the Assyrian Empire was Ashur. They worshipped the god Ashur and considered him as their main god. The Assyrians built big and beautiful palaces for their kings.

Many historians believe that the Neo-Assyrian Empire was the first true empire in the world.

There is more
to know about
the Assyrian
and Neo-
Assyrian Empire.
Research more
and have fun!

Visit
BABY PROFESSOR
EDUCATION KIDS
www.BabyProfessorBooks.com
to download Free Baby Professor eBooks
and view our catalog of new and exciting
Children's Books